One of Britain's leading graphologists, Gloria Hargreaves
has assisted companies around the world in the selection of
personnel, and regularly undertakes lecture tours on the
QE2. She has published a number of books and magazine
articles, and has also appeared on television.

Also by Gloria Hargreaves

A DICTIONARY OF GRAPHOLOGY (with Peggy Wilson)
The A–Z of Your Personality

THE LOVERS' HANDBOOK
Handwriting and Personal Relationships

GLORIA
HARGREAVES

How They Write

*Secrets of the famous revealed
by a leading graphologist*

PETER OWEN
London

For Fred, Edward, Frank and Marie

PETER OWEN PUBLISHERS
73 Kenway Road London SW5 0RE

First published in Great Britain 1991
© Gloria Hargreaves 1991

A catalogue record for this book is available from the British Library

ISBN 0-7206-0838-4

Printed in Great Britain by Billings of Worcester

INTRODUCTION

When we first learn to write we conform to a specific style referred to by graphologists as 'copybook'. This obviously varies from country to country but, providing a graphologist has copies of the various styles taught throughout the world, it should not present a problem. It is the deviation from the original style that sets the graphologist on a wonderful voyage of discovery. All the interpretations are based on an established body of knowledge but much depends on the skill of the particular graphologist in arriving at an interpretation and conveying it in a language that is clearly understood.

Graphology can reveal the writer's individuality, originality, leadership qualities, motivation, intelligence, tastes and interests, ability to overcome day-to-day obstacles, and very much more. The dominant movements in handwriting that lead us to our interpretations are the size, slant, speed, pressure, forms of connection, angularity, roundness, broadness, narrowness, layout, spacing and, to a lesser extent, the individual letter forms. The personal pronoun 'I' plays its own particular part, as do the 'i' dots and 't' crosses.

Many of you will say, 'I never write the same way twice!' The dominants change little but mood changes which result in a slightly different appearance to the layman are easily detected by the trained eye of the graphologist. There are times when one sees a great deterioration in the handwriting movements and these are readily recognised as periods of great stress, bereavement or illness. Character traits that deviate from the considered norm will instantly show up in the handwriting.

Graphology is used widely not only by individuals wishing to gain greater insight into their own personality but also by companies wishing to employ the most suitable applicants. It is also used in vocational and marriage guidance, in education and in crime detection. It is practised throughout Europe and the United

States, where it is an established academic subject taught in universities. It does, however, have its limitations. Age, for example, cannot be judged with total accuracy. A person's actual age is often at variance with his mental age. How often have we heard the remark, 'That child was born old' or, 'Will he/she ever grow up?' The sex of a person can also present problems. Men may have feminine traits and women may have masculine ones. What is certain is that we are all a mixture of both. Since age and sex have a bearing on character analysis, it is always wise to establish these from the outset. Handwriting can tell you nothing about the future but it can indicate the writer's potential and enable you to give an estimate of his future performance.

Like a fingerprint, every person's handwriting is unique to them. Most of us will recognise the handwriting of our friends and relatives on envelopes as they drop through the letter box. The famous people in this book have all left, or are leaving, their mark in the world and the most dominant and interesting factor to be found in their handwriting is that they all possess a mixture of positive and negative traits. They are just like you and I.

My special thanks to those many people who, during my twelve years of cruising around the world lecturing on graphology, have provided me with the samples and the opportunity to analyse the handwriting of the rich and famous.

Gloria Hargreaves

SCIENCE AND THE ARTS

Maria Callas
Opera Singer

This lady had one way of working and one way only – she showed consistency, a systematic approach to everything she undertook and the desire to complete any task in a logical manner. All of this is seen in the total connectedness of the script. She had a great dislike of interruption until she felt she had come to a proper stopping point. The whole shows dedication, steadfastness and an explosive nature confirmed by the erratic pressure.

Sir Colin Davis
Conductor

The very thick stroke of the creative artist. Angular movements show a lot of mental energy and the comma 'i' dot shows curiosity and observation. The script is totally connected, revealing the writer to be very logical and quite compulsive. He is restless and needs stimulation to avoid boredom. A challenge has great appeal to him. He is an extremely mature and intelligent individual. The final 's' shows originality in thought and action, and the rising signature indicates professional ambition.

Jerome Kern
Composer

This totally disconnected script falls into a very creative category. This is the writing of an inspired individualist who personally was egocentric, somewhat insecure and rather moody. He was also intuitive and very much open to the influences of the moment. He was super-sensitive, as shown by the extremely light pressure, and took offence easily. He could be stubborn and uncooperative. His signature, which is larger than the script, suggests that he presented a far more extroverted personality than was indeed the fact.

Wolfgang Amadeus Mozart
Composer

A signature that looks as if it has been executed with a paint-brush. This intensely passionate individual became totally

absorbed in anything he undertook. He was extremely hot-blooded and sensual. He delighted in nature and all it had to offer. The sickle-like shape at the bottom of the 'z' shows a certain sadistic streak and the whole shows undisciplined daydreaming and sexual fantasy.

Sergei Vassilievich Rachmaninoff
Composer and pianist

This totally disconnected handwriting speaks of the writer's wealth of creative and original ideas which continually inspired and filled his mind. An extraordinarily intuitive individual, who had the ability to make decisions instantly, he was endowed with an unusual imagination and was given to meditation, dreams and premonitions. He was witty, had great presence of mind, and could well have succeeded in the literary world. Poetry was one of his great loves. He was prone to spells of moodiness, outbursts of temper, and tantrums. He had a tendency to break off social relationships for no apparent reason. He loved beauty in all its shapes and forms.

Dame Joan Sutherland
Opera singer

A lady who tries to maintain an optimistic front at all times but does not always succeed, as shown by the bowed base to her signature. The writing is quite rounded, indicating a kindly, pleasant nature, and the full loops suggest emotional outbursts. She is sometimes secretive (note the closed 'o's and 'a's) and communicates best with those known well to her. The pull of the final 'd', used as an underline, hints at her pride in previous successes rather than looking to the future with confidence.

Thomas Alva Edison
Inventor

This fascinating, extremely squared writing tells of a material-istic individual who liked possessions for the sense of security they brought him. It also shows that he was logical, practical and thoroughly enjoyed working with his hands. He was independent and had difficulty in relating his thoughts and ideas to other people. His very accurately placed 'i' dots speak of his obsession with detail, whilst those elongated 't' crosses reveal his great will power and ability to overcome any obstacle. A man who would not let up. A cold personality but a brilliant mind.

Albert Einstein
Physicist and mathematician

This very tiny handwriting tells us of an introverted, shy and reserved individual who had no wish to appear in the limelight. He could work for hours alone on a project and his powers of concentration were tremendous. Every 'i' is dotted, every 't' is crossed with great precision, showing his concern for accuracy in all things. The evenness of the word and line spacing shows his absolute clarity of thought and painstaking desire to be thorough and consistent. He was receptive to ideas from other people (indicated by the breadth of the writing) but was basically a loner who felt overrated when given any praise. The extremely large 't' crossing in 'Einstein' suggests a protective attitude towards others.

Sir Alexander Fleming
Discoverer of penicillin

The small handwriting that denotes the scientific mind. These are the thinkers of the world rather than the doers. The

I have no use for them

Alexander Fleming

writer could concentrate for long periods of time on a project, as seen by the complete connectedness of the letters. The small personal pronoun 'I' indicates he was a very modest man, but the slightly larger signature suggests that he liked to appear more confident. The unusual little hooked starting stroke on the 'h' shows how he held on to ideas and didn't give up easily, while the 'i' dot to the far right reveals both impatience and curiosity. The curl on the capital 'F' shows he was proud of his achievements.

Sigmund Freud
Originator of psychoanalysis

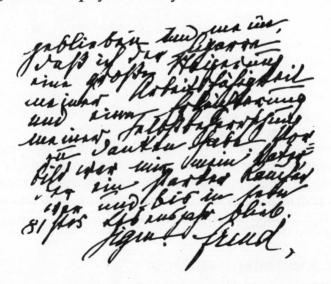

A man of high ideals, as shown by the tall upper loops, who was frequently disappointed in his fellow humans. (Note the falling words at the ends of lines.) At times he became quite

12

melancholy. He was basically introverted and compulsive in his behavioural patterns. It is an angular script, showing mental energy. This was someone who did not often change his ideas. The upward-pointing strokes reveal his desire for recognition and achievement on a mental level, but resentment towards past events in his life is also in evidence. Some breaks between letters indicate intuition and perception, whilst his sharp strokes show he could size up situations easily and had a quick grasp of facts. He experienced difficulty in relating intimately to his own sex.

Jeffrey Archer
Popular-fiction writer

The rather gate-like construction of the signature tells us of a man who puts up barriers and obstacles. He dislikes anyone prying into his moods or motives. This is both an analytical and a calculating script. Because of the variation in the letter sizes at the ends of words, we see someone who can change from discretion to complete tactlessness. The 'n' in 'reading' shows his enquiring mentality, whilst the simplicity of the letter formations tells of his direct approach to solving problems. The swinging, large movements in the lower zone indicate a need for change and variety in his sex life. He is also quite materialistic.

Robert Browning
Poet

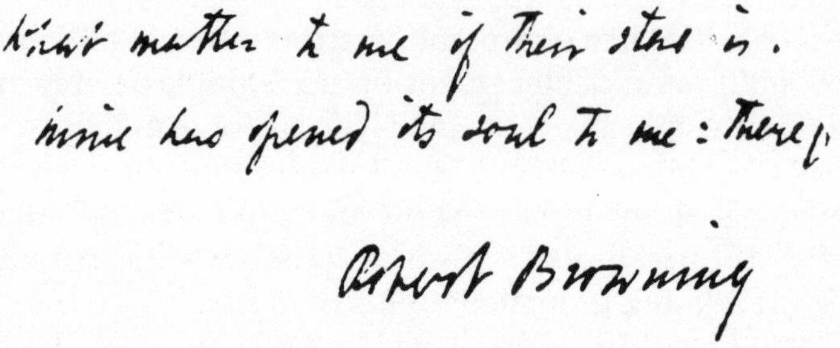

[handwritten text, illegible]

Robert Browning

The light pressure and sharp writing show a sensitive individual who was critical both of himself and others. He was quite obsessive about cleanliness and had a cold, remote manner. Spiritual and idealistic, he was disappointed with his fellow humans and felt in many ways that he did not fit in. He was not gifted with a high energy level but saved what energy he had until it was needed. He could have a sharp tongue, as shown by the small, pointed 't' crosses. A man who took offence very easily.

Barbara Cartland
Romantic novelist

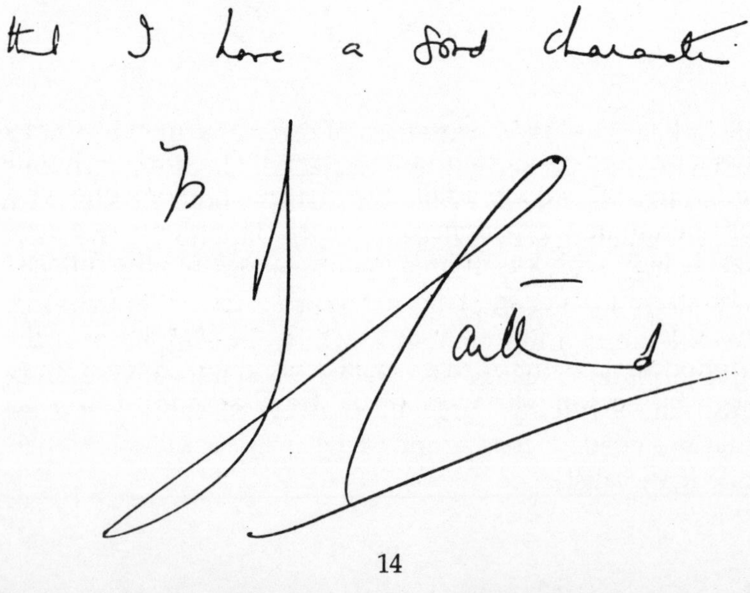

[handwritten text] that I love a good character

[signature]

The enormous signature clearly shows the writer's love of recognition and of being in the public eye. Underneath, however, is a very private person who enjoys time alone and who is capable of working for long periods alone on a project, as confirmed by the small middle-zone letters. She is logical, works steadily and dislikes interruptions en route. She is idealistic (tall upper-zone letters) and is frequently disappointed that others do not share the high standards she expects of herself. She likes food, as shown by the open top on the 'g' in 'good'. Despite her success the very large spaces between the words indicate feelings of isolation and of being out of step with the rest of the world. (*Shown slightly reduced.*)

Agatha Christie
Detective-story writer

A very clearly written signature with many breaks between letters, showing a lot of intuition. The opening at the top of the 'A' indicates quite a talkative nature and someone who was open to new experiences or ideas. The writer was a very likeable lady with lots of imagination, as seen in the fullness of the letters. She was broad-minded and uninhibited. A generous nature is revealed, as is a degree of quiet confidence, shown by the small underline. A charming, delightful person who was honest, frank and direct.

Charles Dickens
Novelist

The ornate 'C' hints at vulgarity and ostentation, which is confirmed by the excessive underlining of the name. The 'i' in 'Dickens', written like an 'e', suggests pseudo charm, and the large middle-zone letters suggest a rather self-centred individual who made great issue of trivial matters. He worked well in a systematic manner but he was difficult to get along with. He placed great emphasis on personal appearance and was quite highly sexed with a very visual mind.

F. Scott Fitzgerald
Novelist

A rather artistic signature showing creativity and imagination. From its large size we can see that the writer liked being involved in large-scale projects and had ambition and a high energy level. He had a desire, too, for tactile stimulation and a need for physical closeness with others. A deep capacity for the enjoyment of new experiences is also in evidence. The script is quite disconnected, which suggests he used a lot of intuition in his projects. The strokes are firm and indicate both self-assurance and a good sense of timing. A positive individual who could at times be very adamant. Warm natured but somewhat repressed sexually.

W. Somerset Maugham
Writer

little white folds.
ocean and for a
tired wings.

W. Somerset Maugham

A tactful individual, as seen by the decreasing letters at the ends of the words. The slight slant to the right shows the writer's desire to communicate his feelings and ideas to others, and the 'i' dots, again always to the right, show how impatient and frustrated he could be as his thoughts came to him quicker than he could write them down. It's a connected script, revealing him to be logical and able to work for long periods at a time alone on a project. In fact, he strongly disliked interruptions. The very consistent word and line spacing indicate a man who was organised and planned his time well and effectively. Some lovely connecting strokes between the words 'white' and 'folds' tell us of his original thinking. This is the writing of an uncomplicated individual who thoroughly enjoyed using his mental talents to the full.

John Mortimer
Novelist and playwright

This writer is very intelligent with a great deal of mental energy, as revealed by the angular movements. Firmness,

Charlie
up for flights of stars
with love
John Osborne

inflexibility and determination are all confirmed by the heavy pressure. This is the handwriting of a blunt-spoken individual who hates to have his moods or motives questioned. A lot of pride and a strong ego are shown in the largeness of the signature, and the 'p' in 'up' indicates stubbornness.

George Bernard Shaw
Dramatist and critic

G: Bernard Shaw

This small script reveals a man of considerable ability, one who did not seek approval for his words or actions and had good powers of concentration. Some of the letters are ink-filled, showing he could be explosive, and the long hook at the end of 'Shaw' indicates that he held very firmly to his ideas and possessions. It is a narrow script, suggesting that he was tense and somewhat sceptical. Any wastage of time or materials irritated him. He was gifted at solving abstract problems but had little understanding of the emotions of those close to him. A man who was fond of studying and reading till the end of his days. (*Signature shown enlarged.*)

Oscar Wilde
Writer and wit

A very broad, simplified script without :.ny superfluous strokes whatsoever. A great freedom lover who had little desire for personal possessions, this writer needed space, travel, large rooms in which to spread himself, and had a ready acceptance of new ideas and experiences. He was tolerant and accepted others for what they were. His energy level was not high but he paced himself well in order to prolong his staying power. His ideas were very personal and often quite inventive. There is no hint of aggression or anger in his writing. His motto in life was 'live and let live'.

Salvador Dali
Artist

A very difficult personality and one given to many changes of mood, as indicated by the variable letter sizes. He was both inspired and rebellious. He liked behaving in an unacceptable manner and delighted in shocking people. He was gifted and original in his thinking, but day-to-day responsibilities remained a mystery to him. He could be very sarcastic (sharp letter formations), persistent (knotted 't's) and tactless in the extreme. A creative individual who worked in fits and starts.

His emotional nature was erratic and he was completely undisciplined. The large signature tells us he was in love with himself but had little understanding of what made him tick!

Henry Moore
Sculptor

The angularity of this signature tells of a keen, agile mind, and the roundness of the 'o's in 'Moore' reveals kindness towards his fellow humans. Yet the whole suggests a demanding nature – one that was not easily satisfied. This writer was a great striver and rarely pleased with his efforts. The last, falling stroke on the 'e' suggests he felt disappointed with some of his past relationships. A very intelligent and mature individual, he could at times be quite morose.

Pablo Picasso
Artist

A simple and aesthetic signature reveals clear, if unusual, thinking processes. This was a man who disliked clutter. His great imagination is shown in the very large 'P', and its irregular formation indicates a certain rebelliousness. He behaved without face or façade and didn't really care whether other people liked him or not. He had tremendous intuition and relied totally upon it. A poetic individual.

Walt Disney
Film producer and cartoonist

An imaginative and emotional individual, as shown by the large loops and capital letters. There is a great deal of originality to every movement of the writing, clearly indicating an innovative and creative person who delighted in his talent. The pressure shows warmth and a sense of fun. The loops on the 'n' show he could be charming even to those he did not like, but the knotted 'a' is a sign of secretiveness – he would convey his ideas to others only when he chose to. The whole reveals his love of fun, a sense of humour and a great intensity of feeling.

Sir Alfred Hitchcock
Film director

A very speedy, quick-flowing script showing an agile mind and rapidity of thought. All the letters are linked together, revealing great powers of concentration. The writer did everything according to his own ideas and was not bound in any way by convention. He was exacting, persistent and always carried his plans through to the end. The connectedness of the words and the large lower loops show how he delighted in exercising his power of artistic expression. He also had a well-developed appreciation of music. An impulsive man who sometimes squandered his wealth unnecessarily. His sex drive was also quite powerful and tact was not his strong point.

Florence Nightingale
'The Lady with the Lamp'

A kindly person who pushed herself to the limit. The left-slanting downward stroke on the 'y' shows this writer sub-limated her sex drive in the service of others, but she was also very progressive, as seen by the pull of the writing to the right. Tomorrow was all-important to her. She liked people and liked to communicate with them, was proud, idealistic and very demonstrative. She could be impulsive, overtaxed herself and, at times, suffered periods of exhaustion. The funny curl on the 'F' in 'Florence' shows her reaching up for inspiration and suggests a sense of humour, too. She was a brave lady but not always practical and rather inclined to overreact. She did not always absorb or learn from past experiences.

John Young
Astronaut

The leanness of the writer's strokes tells of his technical training, while the loop on 'John' shows his thoroughness. The rising signature confirms his professional ambition. Note that the first stroke on 'John' is amazingly like the nose cone of an aircraft, done completely subconsciously! The full lower loops show a very high energy level and strong materialistic and sexual interests. The connectedness of the script indicates

John Young

his logical approach to life and his ability to work in a very systematic manner. His powers of concentration are excellent.

POLITICS

James Callaghan
Prime Minister (1976–1979)

Well begun is half done! — Or as they used to say.

Anyway congratulations on what you have managed so far.

Jim Callaghan

The fairly light pressure of this script shows that the writer is not gifted naturally with an abundance of energy. However the general regularity of the handwriting suggests consistency of effort, and the quick movement across the page indicates speedy and agile mental processes. The absence of angular letter forms shows his desire to settle problems by conciliatory means. A dislike of noise and aggression is also in evidence. The baseline is a little too flexible: he may allow himself to be influenced too much by other people. His letters are a mixture of broadness, revealing courage and directness, and narrowness, showing caution and restraint. One feels he could have achieved a lot more in his lifetime. His signature says that he conducts himself the same in public as in private.

Sir Winston Churchill
Prime Minister (1940–1945; 1951–1955)

Know, according to the in your department. dates on which all Dreadnoughts, built have been (a) order (c) launched (d)

A very simplified handwriting showing a high degree of intellectual discipline. The writer's skill as a leader is seen in his foresight (letters moving clearly to the right), orderliness and quick grasp of essentials. The sharp 't' crosses tell of his strong will and directness. The regular, even strokes show his ability to concentrate, plus a sense of order and punctuality. He was industrious, persevering and conscientious. The excellent word and line spacing clearly indicate his great planning and organising ability. He was a good decision maker and was indifferent to what others thought about him.

Edward Heath
Prime Minister (1970–1974)

The simplicity of the strokes indicates efficiency and a desire for truth and accuracy. This person keeps his emotions under control and is direct in his manner of speaking. The script is quite broad and shows his expansiveness in social situations; however he is always on his guard and can appear formal and cold. His musical talent is revealed by the first stroke of the 'H' in 'Heath'. The large capitals show a lot of pride and the underlining denotes self-assurance, although the small letters hint at a certain reserve. He is a quietly confident man who tends to stand back and watch rather than push himself to the forefront.

Michael Heseltine
Conservative politician

A totally disconnected script, showing that this writer's opinions are based on instinct rather than logic. He has a brilliant and original mind and great literary talents. He can grasp essentials instantly and act upon them. He is very critical of himself and others and is particularly sensitive, often taking offence when none is intended. He is egocentric, moody and restless. The very wide spacing between his words indicates feelings of isolation; he can even feel lonely in a crowded room. He fears contact and closeness with

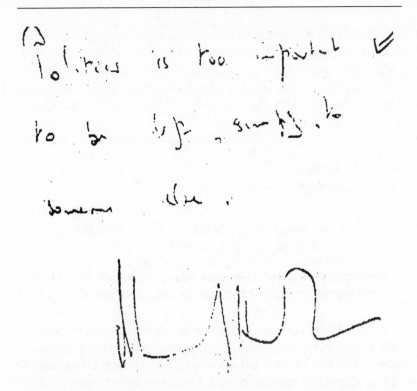

others. From the large spaces between the lines it can be seen that he has difficulty in trusting his fellow men. However, he holds himself in high esteem. His illegible signature confirms all of the above.

Douglas Hurd
Conservative politician

A direct, honest, likeable and articulate person who nevertheless plays his cards close to his chest. This is shown by the rounded base to his letters and the angular tops. The reversed 'd' tells us he is very self-protective and quick to defend himself and his opinions. The whole shows him as hard-working, loyal and sincere. Reliability is seen in the even baseline, and literary ability in the breaks between letters. Charm runs throughout: a soft exterior but quite tough underneath.

Neil Kinnock
Leader of the Labour party

A speedy script which shows a quick-thinking individual with a high degree of mental and physical energy. The sharp points on the 'm's reveal a critical and investigative mind which explores and digs for knowledge, always asking questions and seeking answers. He is impetuous in his expression of emotion, as seen by the frequent connection of his letters. He is thorough, systematic and persistent, and aims to see things through to a successful conclusion – even, at times, to the bitter end. However, he can get bogged down with detail and can miss the overall meaning. His firm, long 't' crosses show his protectiveness towards his family and colleagues alike. Job satisfaction is more important to him than material gain. There is little energy left over for sexual pursuits (small endstrokes on 'y's) but otherwise he makes a kindly, affectionate partner.

John Major
Prime Minister (1990–)

The very tall upper-zone letters tell us that this is a man of intelligence and ambition, but because it is a narrow script we

John Major

know he is never satisfied with his own achievements. He always feels the need to prove himself and has a demanding conscience and uncompromising ideas of right and wrong. The small middle-zone letters indicate someone of great independence who does not seek the approval of others and who is not particularly concerned about his popularity. Firm downstrokes show a good sense of timing and the whole suggests that he is economical and has a dislike of wastefulness. He is a loyal, honest and reliable man with a dry sense of humour. Great responsibility could take its toll on his health, as he becomes tense and nervous under pressure but will never show it. (*Shown slightly reduced.*)

Sir Denis Thatcher
Businessman; husband of Margaret Thatcher

Indeed say't anything for publication. "I" is

Denis Thatcher

Margaret chose well when she picked Denis as her partner. The good pressure tells us that he is a warm, affectionate and supportive husband. He can also be very stubborn and follow his own interests and hobbies no matter who objects! He is a lover of nature and kindly to people less fortunate than himself. He has a generosity of spirit and considerable charm. This is very positive handwriting indicating business acumen, and the strong 'p' shows how he follows his ideas through. Some of the ovals are slightly ink-filled, so he likes a tipple and good food. He has a colourful imagination and, on occasions, is prone to explosive outbursts, but he is warm-natured and sublimates some of his sexual energy in good deeds. His signature shows materialism.

Margaret Thatcher
Prime Minister (1979–1990)

A very quick script showing speed of thought, energy and progressive thinking. The simplification of the letter formations indicates the writer's direct approach and a desire to simplify issues. She loathes waffle of any type and has a great capacity for the quick grasp, comprehension and assimilation of essentials. A combination of connected and disconnected strokes shows she is capable of a happy mixture of imagination and intelligence to put her vision into effect and make her dreams come true. Negatively, she is very intolerant of those who disagree with her and does not make a good listener. Her signature reveals her to be genuine; she believes in every word she utters. Sexually, she is always in a hurry, needs little sleep and has a clinical approach to this area of her life. She probably enjoys playing the piano just as much!

Sir Harold Wilson
(Baron Wilson of Rievaulx)
Prime Minister (1964–1970; 1974–1976)

LONDON. SW₁

They tried to tell us we're too young.
But they were wrong, weren't they?
Best wishes,
Harold Wilson.

The smallness here tells of this writer's capacity for accuracy and his aptitude for detailed and scientific work. His powers of concentration are excellent, plus he has an extremely retentive memory. He is a thinker rather than a doer, a particularly clever individual who could be somewhat manipulative. Despite his shyness and reserve, bordering on an inferiority complex, he has quite a power drive. A man of great ability who appears to have been held back by a lack of self-confidence. The ink-filled ovals suggest he can be explosive at times and has a liking for a tipple!

George Bush
President of the United States (1989–)

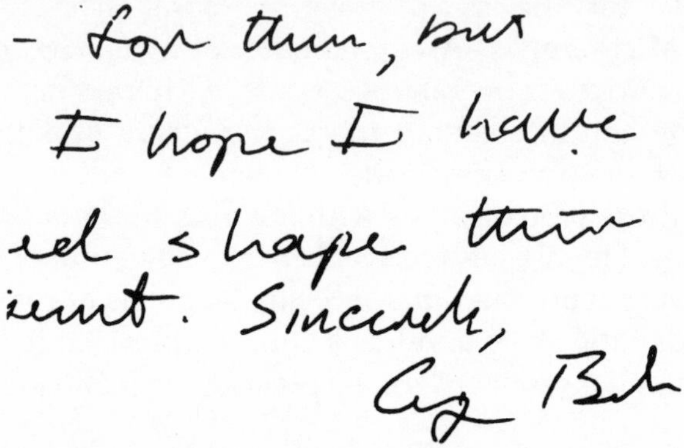

[handwritten text]

— for them, but
I hope I have
ed shape thin
ient. Sincerely,
Geo Bush

This script shows a man with a quick, alert mind, but because of the uneven baseline it also indicates that he can become excitable and, at times, moody. He is very versatile, impatient and progressive. The pointed tops on the 'm' and 'n' reveal his penetrating intelligence and his ability to simplify issues and come to rapid conclusions. The majority of his 'o's and 'a's are closed, showing discretion, and diplomacy and tact are strongly indicated by the decrease in the size of the letters at the ends of words. He does not possess a high energy level so has to take care to pace himself well. The printed 'I', in an otherwise cursive script, speaks of great independence and clear original thinking. Ball games appeal to him.

Jimmy Carter
President of the United States (1977–1981)

The many breaks between the letters here reveal a man whose judgements are based on intuition. He has the ability to size up situations quickly and is very observant. The rising lines are a sign of enthusiasm, but the script is a little too right-slanting, which indicates strong emotional reactions and impulsiveness. Some memory lapses are shown by the unexplained large gaps between letters. It is a fast script suggesting a quick mind and directness. A progressive,

The beautiful book & lighter will always remind me of your hospitality –

Jimmy

inspired individual who experiences difficulty in controlling his emotional reactions. He is quick to take offence and often feels restless and unsettled.

Edward Kennedy
Democrat politician

Edward. M. Kennedy

The pressure here is very variable, indicating moodiness and erratic working patterns, but the simplicity of the strokes reveals efficiency and the ability to recognise essentials. When the writer applies himself, therefore, he works extremely well; at other times, he seems disinterested. The small middle-zone letters speak of difficulty in delegating and of lack of trust in others. The abrupt finish on the 'd' in 'Edward' tells of disappointments in personal relationships. The signature falls and rises, indicating that he wishes to appear enthusiastic but does not always succeed. The X-like 'y' in the surname, which is also found in Robert Kennedy's signature, suggests a fear of death.

Jacqueline (Kennedy) Onassis
First Lady of the United States (1961–1963)

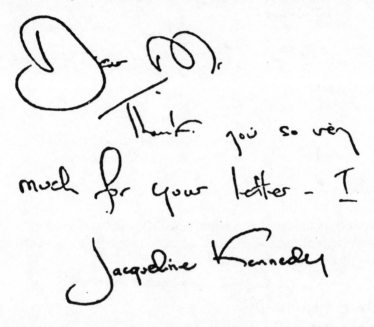

The simple strokes show great intelligence and their height speaks of an idealistic lady with a strong spiritual leaning. It is a slightly left-slanting script, revealing sensitivity but also indicating a person who can be charming outwardly whilst inwardly remaining aloof. The very small middle-zone letters tell of her creative ability but also reveal that she was not content on a day-to-day basis. The large 'k' in 'Thank' speaks of some rebelliousness. There are a lot of disconnected letters that reveal great intuition and the ability to size up situations very quickly. Negatively, the 'K' in 'Kennedy' tells of a condescending attitude.

John F. Kennedy
President of the United States (1961–1963)

The speed of the writing indicates an extremely quick-thinking and agile mind. The letters decrease in size at the ends of words, showing tact, diplomacy and manipulative qualities. This thready type of writing is identified with very high intelligence, broad vision and original ideas, but the 't' crossings vary in length revealing unpredictability. An impatient individual who drove himself and others hard, and had a high energy level and sex drive.

Robert F. Kennedy
Democrat statesman

This hastily written script reveals an alert, speedy mind and a high energy level. The firm downstrokes show the enthusiasm the writer brought to anything he became interested in. He had a warm, sensual nature but could be sarcastic and cutting in his remarks. The thickness of the downstrokes shows he was very self-centred and had a quick temper. He also had a great deal of energy for sporting and sexual pursuits. The writing is narrow, indicating that he frequently felt inhibited and restrained, which in turn made him frustrated and angry. The X-like 'y' in 'Kennedy' clearly shows fear of death and confirms that he was disappointed in his achievements.

Martin Luther King
American civil-rights leader

This right-slanting script shows an individual who looked to the future, but the starting stroke on the 'M' and the hook on the 't' cross tell us that he took many ideas from the past along with him. Leadership qualities and idealism are shown by the size, and the loops reveal great emotion. He could laugh and cry easily and readily gave vent to his feelings. This man overreacted to situations and had quite a power complex. Energetic and stubborn, he held firmly to his ideas. He needed recognition and acted with boldness and optimism. Negatively he could be boastful and dogmatic.

Abraham Lincoln
President of the United States (1860–1865)

Extremely balanced writing which shows good, sound judgement. It is also very connected, indicating the writer's progressive and logical ideas. He worked well, systematically and with great concentration and attention to detail. His letters are firm, showing a good sense of timing, and the evenness of the baseline speaks of reliability and emotional stability. Not the most inspired man but a man of integrity, honesty and directness. He believed in everything he said; he was a good decision maker and was discreet and caring in his use of words. There is only one sign of rebelliousness and that is in the split 'k' in 'know'. A very trustworthy, honest man, who suffered with some pain in his fingers.

Richard Nixon
President of the United States (1969–1974)

The first signature, taken from early in the writer's career, shows a very logical individual, someone who had a clear goal in sight and was persistent. He was also well-balanced, honest, reliable and dedicated to every task in hand. His mind was filled with curiosity, and his desire to lead was great, as shown by the large capitals and the connectedness. His loops show he was emotionally healthy and quick-thinking.

By the time he left office, his signature had disintegrated to an illegible line; he obviously felt he had lost control. He was still clinging on desperately, as seen by the hooked 'i' dot. He was also experiencing difficulty in communicating with those around him and could not be pinned down to a particular course of action.

Ronald Reagan
President of the United States (1981–1989)

The great simplicity of the capitals indicates the writer's pride and ambition; their largeness is the sign of a showman. The gap after the first 'R' reveals his power of observation, and the slightly old-fashioned style his respect for tradition. The connectedness tells us that he is objective and purposeful in his attitudes. The whole suggests an ordinary 'Mr Nice Guy', who is idealistic but often suspicious of the moods and

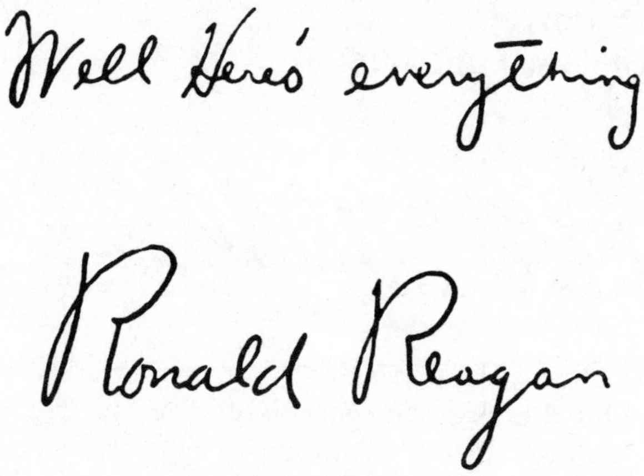

Well Here's everything

Ronald Reagan

motives of those around him. He does not have a great imagination and the very high 't' cross reveals that some of his ideas are not based on practicality!

Fidel Castro
Prime Minister of Cuba (1959–)

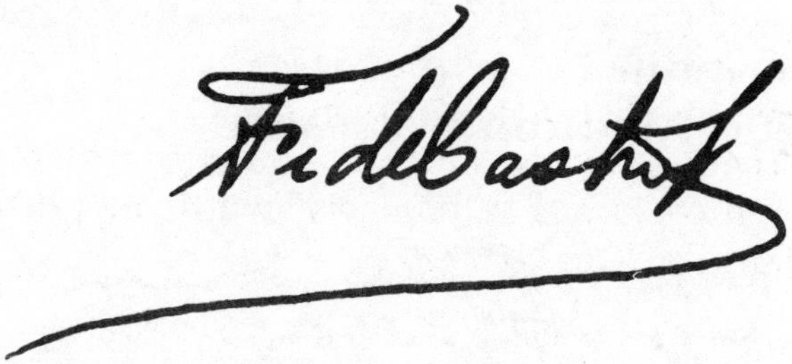

Fidel Castro

A flamboyant, attention-seeking individual is shown here. He is very domineering, as seen by the large, extended top on the 'F' in 'Fidel'. The hard angles reveal someone who greatly dislikes interference of any type. The heavy pressure shows a high energy level, a strong will and a forceful personality. A very proud, self-opinionated man who can, just occasionally, show some softness. This is indicated by the rounded capital 'C' in 'Castro'. He uses harshness and forcefulness to dominate and control others. A very strong personality whose desire is to leave his mark on the environment.

Oliver Cromwell
Lord Protector (1653–1658)

This large, angular script speaks of the writer's leadership qualities, mental energy and self-righteousness. The angularity also reveals that the complexity of human emotion baffled him and any appeal made to him had to be based on logic. He thrived on facts. He was both compulsive and a perfectionist. His pen never left the paper during the penning of this signature, revealing his stubbornness and his desire always to have the last word. He expected others to follow him without question, but the varying pressure tells of erratic outbursts and a lack of consistency in decision making. His ego was huge.

Mahatma Gandhi
Indian political and spiritual leader

A kindly, strong individual who needed to be with people, as shown by the closeness of the personal pronoun 'I' to the word 'am'. Innovative thinking is indicated by the connections between the words 'to', 'send' and 'you'. There is both rebelliousness and humility in the script. The broadness tells of his great courage and also of his need for space. The 'p' in 'copies' hints at stubbornness. His powers of concentration were excellent and his approach to problem solving very original. A particularly gifted man, whose rising signature reveals his ambition and humour. The wavy underlining suggests that he needed to have the last word but did not always expect to be taken seriously.

Charles de Gaulle
President of France (1959–1969)

The smallness of the script indicates great powers of concentration and very good attention to detail. At times this writer was impatient, and the heavy final full stop at the end of his signature tells us that he liked to have the last word. He was in many respects a reserved individual who welcomed time alone. The speed of the writing indicates his ability to think, act and move quickly. He could be intolerant of those less well informed than himself, and his signature, slightly larger than the script, shows he could behave in a superior manner. Its rising slant also shows his professional ambition. This is the writing of a very clever individual who would have risen to the top in any profession he had chosen.

Heinrich Himmler
Head of the German SS and the Gestapo (1936–1945)

A very aggressive signature showing great inflexibility, determination and rigidity. A man who could not be argued with; his word was law. He had the desire to impose his will on others and harboured feelings of resentment towards society. Considerable energy and vigour is in evidence. He had an aptitude for hard work and thoroughness and enjoyed surmounting obstacles and solving difficult problems. A love of order is shown, as is his ability to plan ahead. A hard, austere man who had a dislike of ease and comfort and was baffled by human emotion. The club-shaped crossing on the first initial shows hostility and aggression.

Adolf Hitler
German Führer (1934–1945)

At the time this signature was written, the writer was trying to maintain an optimistic front, as shown by the arcade shape of the signature, but he was not succeeding. The ink-filled ovals speak of an explosive temperament and one given to excesses in all areas. The letters are very narrow, showing him to be tense, uptight and intolerant. The very involved capital 'H' is a sign of coarseness and vulgarity, and the high 't' cross shows high ideals and sarcasm. The whole suggests an angry, self-doubting and depressed frame of mind.

Karl Marx
Founder of modern Communism

The very small handwriting of the exacting personality who is a perfectionist in everything he does. This writer welcomed the chance to work alone for long periods of time and was happiest when unobserved. He had an academic mentality

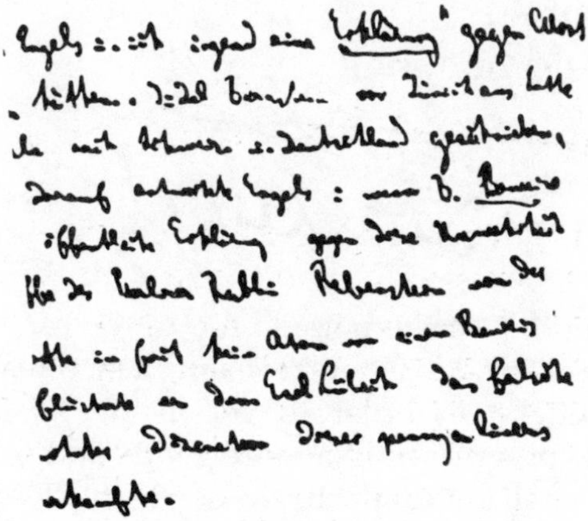

[handwritten note in German]

and was unconcerned about what others thought of him. He was very persistent (some knotted letters), pedantic and, on occasions, uptight and explosive. Some leftward movements show he was strongly influenced by the past. He experienced difficulty in relating intimately in close relationships.

Napoleon I (Napoleon Bonaparte)
Emperor of the French (1804–1815)

The smeary, thick pressure shows an indulgence of sensuality and, with the falling line, indicates a temperamental, rather depressed individual. The small letters reveal feelings of inferiority but the great underline shows how he compensated for this by behaving in an arrogant, aggressive and attention-seeking manner. He was explosive, single-minded and either silent or overly effusive. Everything about him was intense and distrustful. A man who was determined to make his mark.

Erwin Rommel
German field marshal

With the exception of the pointed top to the capital 'R', we have a series of rounded letters revealing a man who could be aggressive initially in order to get his way but, having achieved that, progressed in a more gentle and co-operative manner. The small loop at the beginning of the 'R' shows him pondering, then the forcefulness of his personality follows. He was undoubtedly a very good leader; see how one stroke gently leads to another, showing how he encouraged and praised others. A logical man and a stubborn one. His final 'l' shows he was in control. The huge top on the 'R' indicates a certain protectiveness.

Joseph Stalin
Soviet leader (1922–1953)

The thick, smeary pressure shows a great intensity of feeling, a vivid imagination and overindulgence of sensuality. The lack of an outlet for this writer's very high energy levels resulted in cruelty, intolerance, brutality and sadism, all confirmed by the club-like strokes at the ends of letters. It is a pedantic type of script, indicating obsessiveness, narrow-mindedness and anger. Explosive outbursts are shown in the ink-filled letters and these would be followed by bouts of silence and depression. A very difficult personality who could not be reasoned with.

Pierre Trudeau
Prime Minister of Canada
(1968–1979; 1980–1984)

A difficult-to-read signature showing a private individual who does not want his innermost thoughts penetrated. It is a speedy, intelligent script and one that shows a calculating mind capable of great tact and diplomacy. It also reveals that he can see into the minds of others but still keep his own thoughts and position hidden. The loop on the 'd' speaks of thoroughness and the large capitals of pride and conceit. A very capable, manipulative individual. This is quite a phallic signature.

Eamon de Valera
President of the Irish Republic (1959–1973)

A very competent, direct and honest person is revealed in the simplicity and clarity of this signature. It shows a good balance between rounded and squared connecting strokes, indicating emotional stability, good powers of observation and an enquiring mentality. The whole shows maturity, imagination and intelligence. The pointed 'm's reveal his penetrating mind and quick grasp of facts. A genuine individual who searched constantly for the truth. The capitals point to good taste and a love of the arts.

POPULAR MUSIC

Adam Ant
Lead singer, Adam and the Ants

Adam Ant

The quite strong pressure here shows a fairly high energy level, and the clear letter formations indicate efficiency and directness. A slight right slant says that the writer enjoys communicating with others but, from the closed 'a', we can see that he is selective in what he has to say. It's a very legible signature, stating 'I am what I am, take it or leave it.' The size is fairly large so he copes well with being in the public eye, but the raised first stroke on the 'n' in 'Ant' reveals that there is something in his day-to-day life that he finds difficult to handle.

John Lennon
Rock musician and songwriter; member of The Beatles

This writer was a moody, restless individual who would invade other people's time and space but was reluctant to give of his own. The erratic baseline shows he could be indecisive, lacking in will power and even, at times, confused between reality and illusion. He had a tendency to be

*This is my story both humble an
take it to pieces and mend it wil*

John Lennon

influenced by others with stronger personalities. He was
protective of his family and friends but quite rebellious
towards society at large. His greatest gift was his awareness
of everything around him, combined with accuracy and
precision in his work.

Paul McCartney
Rock musician and songwriter; member
of The Beatles

Paul McCartney

A sensitive, caring and creative individual as indicated by the
light pressure and thin strokes. He can however be very
stubborn – note the straight, long stroke on the capital 'P'.
Innovative thinking is shown by the strokes that rise into the
upper zone. This is the handwriting of a realistic man who
uses all the mental talents available to him. The smallness of
the middle-zone letters suggests very good powers of
concentration and the desire to tie up all detail himself. The
swing of his loops to the left tells us that he relies on his
partner for emotional and sexual strength. Certainly the
cleverest and most down-to-earth of The Beatles.

George Harrison
Rock guitarist; member of The Beatles

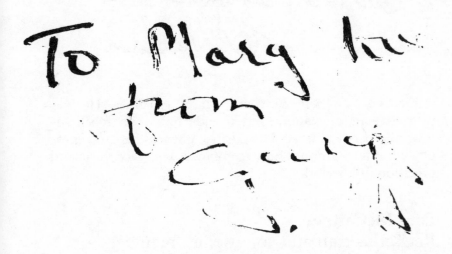

This is very aggressive handwriting indeed, as seen by the repeated angular movements. The 'f' in 'from' tells us the writer has many ideas and gives his all in following them through. The pressure is variable (frequently very heavy), indicating explosive outbursts and mood changes. Basically he has a warm, sensual nature and delights in new experiences. He is very direct and would tell the truth to your face. He is also very physically and materially oriented. A lover of life who is given to hedonism.

Ringo Starr
Drummer; member of The Beatles

This loose, yet connected signature indicates a progressive, unconventional individual who basically does what pleases himself. A certain lack of restraint is seen, together with rebelliousness. Logic, materialism and persistence are all to be found in his powerful 't' crossing. The sharp 'n' shows

a man thirsty for information and knowledge. The unusual
underline shows confidence, humour and a rude gesture!

Max Bygraves
Entertainer

The gentle right slant shows this writer's desire to
communicate his feelings and ideas to others. The 'i' dots are
invariably well placed, revealing great attention to detail, and
the generally connected script indicates his desire to work in
a systematic and well-planned manner. There is little façade
to this man; his handwriting and signature are very similar,
suggesting little difference between his private and public
faces. The 'f's in 'suffice' say he has good ideas and good
follow-through – this is known as the letter of practicality.
There are a lot of strokes moving in three directions,
confirming his great sense of humour, but some movements
suggest that he can be unforgiving to those he has disagreed
with in the past. A very good friend but a bad enemy.

Dave Clark
Drummer, Dave Clark Five

An aggressive showman with a great sense of humour. This is the writing of a man who is determined to succeed – note the angular 'k' and large capitals – and whose motto is perseverance. The pressure is heavy, indicating a high energy level and the need to make an impression on the world. He is an inspired individual and capable of inspiring others. He varies between script and print, which shows he can be changeable and at times moody, but is always out to achieve. Considerable executive ability is shown.

Jason Donovan
Pop singer and actor

Slanting slightly to the right, this script shows a delightful, pleasant and down-to-earth guy who is as genuine as the image he projects. The pressure indicates a high energy level and the loop at the base of the 's' shows he pushes himself to the limit. This is a balanced script, which tells us that he is a good judge of character, has his feet firmly on the ground and

Yeah, but that's not just appeal is that energy. That's
No I think that probably
that applies to everything --
attractive - that's sort of obvi
complements her. But she h
100% concentration - that's at
working with her. But she is
dialogue at Rome and we l
it with each other. And it'd

has the ability to recognise and make the deals that are the most beneficial to him. Satisfaction and the enjoyment of what he does come high on his list of priorities. His lower loops tell us he is not settled on any particular partner but is cautious and will endeavour to pick someone with the long-term view in mind. He loves his food and admires a well-shaped bum!

Sheena Easton
Pop singer

The large, loose, rather erratic script of a lady with a lot of imagination and leadership qualities. She is happiest when involved in large-scale projects and likes being in the driving seat. Restless and very active, she has many ideas, and her firm, high-placed 't' crosses show she has the will power to put these into effect. The very large signature shows her need for recognition, and the inflated lower loops indicate her love of material things. Her sex drive is also strong. Some letters

pull to the left, which suggests she can be cautious and a little sensitive to criticism. The overall impression is of a capable person who loves her work. She also has acting ability. (*Shown slightly reduced.*)

Gary Glitter
Pop singer

This is what is known as mixed-slant writing, indicating constant mood changes. The writer can be friendly and chatty one day whilst avoiding contact and communication the next. (This trait is commonly found in the handwriting of people who were not shown sufficient affection in their formative years.) We can also see a mixture of print and script, which again confirms mood changes and insecurity about his own public image. Quite a few sharp strokes are in evidence, indicating that he can be sarcastic and cynical but is nevertheless thorough in the tasks he undertakes. The 'i'

NAME: *Gary Glitter the 1ST*
HEIGHT: *5.8* WEIGHT: *Fluctue* SIGN: *Taurus*
BIRTH DATE: *NOT TELL YOU* BIRTHPLACE: *BANBURY*
AMBITION: *To get through I. THINK life, with the greatest of ease!*
TURN-ONS: *Waking up.*

TURN-OFFS: *Falling asleep on the Job.*
FAVOURITE FOOD: *I keep experiencing...*
PREFERRED PERFORMERS: *Exotic taste Read as food*
ALL TIME FAVE SONG: *Read Performers*
FAVOURITE PASTIME: *Fishing, and pulling people as Person on.*
BEST FILMS: *I've only made one*
FAVOURITE READING MATTER: *The WIND + WILL*
FAVOURITE OUTFIT: *EVERY THINGS NEW*
PERFECT EVENING: *ENTERTAINING on-est... either... dinner, or see FAVOURITE*

dots are well placed, showing that he likes to tie up all the details himself. The 't' crosses are quite firm, so he attempts to keep his life on an even keel, although he does not always succeed. He relishes change and variety and has no time for complacency or the mundane. The final swing on the 'r' in 'Glitter' shows he can be a hard taskmaster and sets high standards for both himself and those who work with him. Not an easy partner but always an interesting one.

Elton John
Rock musician and songwriter

A determined and decisive character is exhibited by the lean, straight strokes in this script. A sincere person who is basically serious, shy and, on occasions, irritable. He is a

person of regular habits who likes to deal with others in a straightforward, business-minded and ethical manner. He is firm in his resolve and will do what he wants in spite of the consequences. Material gain gives him a great feeling of security and self-worth, yet he is quite spiritual and idealistic. The whole suggests quiet confidence and directness.

Simon Le Bon
Lead singer, Duran Duran

> Hello, Just thought I'd write.
> to say that we're still alive, a
> an Idea of what we'll be doin
> coming year. After a world tour.
> been virtually non stop since Ma
> in our present over 11A ...

An intelligent, clear-thinking individual who communicates best with people well known to him, as seen by the slight right slant combined with closed 'a's and 'o's. All his 'I's look like musical notes, which confirms his talent for, and love of, music. His loops are full, showing his capacity for a loving sexual relationship, and the baseline is straight and even, indicating a sense of responsibility. The accuracy with which he places his 'i' dots reveals his attentiveness to detail. A well-balanced personality.

Kylie Minogue
Pop singer and actress

so great. they ~~the~~ had a food aswell. It was sty. Mmmmm. Mine was often a flop, but great!! If I did want, yes they would provide

A lovely, cheerful individual who enjoys whatever she is doing at the time, as shown by the uprightness of her handwriting. Today is what matters to her. One of her talents, seen by her rounded baseline, is to remain charming even if she feels she is surrounded by idiots. The large middle-zone letters tell us her assurance borders on presumptuousness and conceit, and she tends to exaggerate trivia. She is self-protective and always has a quick, ready answer, revealed by the reversed 'd'. The looped and knotted 't's show perseverance and tenacity. The whole speaks of a love of movement and activity, and the heavy pressure confirms she has the energy to go with it. The 'y' loops are swinging to the left, showing her sexual restlessness and the need for change and variety.

Elvis Presley
Rock-and-roll singer and originator

The connection of the Christian name with the surname shows this writer's desire to project his own image. He was quite a positive person and was in an optimistic frame of mind at the time of writing this sample. This is shown by the rising 'ley' in 'Presley'. It is a warm, friendly and proud signature. Humour is revealed in the three-way movement of the 'P'. He was emotional, artistic and had a high, restless energy level. His sex drive was strong but because of the pull of the 'y' to the left we know that he relied on a partner for encouragement to express his sexuality.

Cliff Richard
Pop singer

The pressure of this writing shows a lot of warmth and humour. Very simple, clear-cut strokes state that the writer is direct and honest in his dealings with others. The accurately placed 'i' dots and 't' crosses tell us he has an eye for detail, and the disconnected nature of much of the script reveals someone with a lot of intuition, who invariably knows what is right for himself. The cruciform shape of the 't's confirms his religious convictions and the pull of the 'y' to the left suggests that he sublimates his sexual drive in helping other people. A nice, genuine individual.

Roger Whittaker
Popular singer

The large, inflated 'R' of the showman but the small letters of a businessman. This is the handwriting of a quick-thinking, clever man, who outwardly shows a great deal of self-assurance. Because of the smallness of the middle-zone letters, we see someone who likes to keep his finger on the pulse of everything he is involved in. Delegating does not come easily to him and he likes to tie up all the details himself. He has a need for privacy in his personal life and guards his family and friends well. He comes alive on stage but experiences little difficulty in reverting to the role of family

man and father. He requires peace and quiet at home in order
to function at his best when in the public eye.

Toyah Willcox
Rock singer and actress

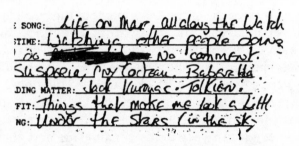

The Greek 'e' shows this writer's love of culture and, combined with the disconnections in her words, reveals literary
ability. This is sharp handwriting indicating a critical nature.
She sets high standards both for herself and those around
her, and is frequently disappointed in her fellow humans,
who are not as thorough as she is. She tends to jump into
situations where a little more preliminary thought would be
a good idea. Her 't' crosses show she can be self-indulgent
and, on occasions, get her priorities wrong. She enjoys
reading, as seen by the printed 's', when she gets the time,
but she experiences some difficulty in relaxing. A clever,
intelligent girl who would benefit from letting go of the past.
She has many good ideas but insufficient follow-through.

George Best
Footballer (Northern Ireland)

The gigantic size of this signature tells of excessive pride; here is someone who must be seen and heard. His tastes lean to the grandiose, luxurious and flamboyant, and he is extravagant, wayward and restless. He is most suited to working in television or the theatre – somewhere he can attract a large audience. Some lack of reality is in evidence. He is a very stubborn man who always feels he knows what is best. His lovely sense of humour is clearly evident, as is his warm and ardent nature. He has a superior attitude but is nonetheless a great showman.

Shirley Crabtree ('Big Daddy')
Wrestler

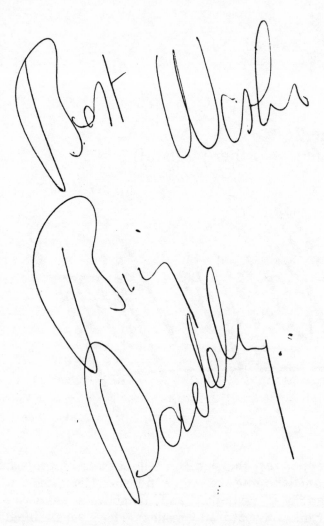

The showman of all showmen! Not one hint of aggression in the whole script. This is a man who thrives on recognition, acclaim and the applause of the audience. The tall upper loops tell of his high intelligence and the preliminary strokes in 'Best', 'Big' and 'Daddy' scream, 'Put me on a platform!' He is quite emotional and would feel genuinely upset if he hurt anyone. A lovely guy with great curiosity, he has good business sense and likes being involved in large-scale projects. (*Shown slightly reduced*.)

Jimmy Greaves
Footballer (England) and television presenter

[handwritten text] to This day for if life · Yesterday is but a dream Left Hand *[signature]*

A very intuitive individual who is better at solving other people's problems than his own. He loves giving advice but is not much good at accepting it! This is predominantly an upright script, which tells us he is self-reliant and has leadership qualities. However, as some of the lower loops pull to the left we can see that he relies on his partner for emotional strength. A close family relationship is very important to him. The many straight strokes indicate efficiency and the desire to be clearly understood. He has a pleasant manner and neither over- nor underestimates his own abilities. His 't' crosses remind one of head-butting but actually reveal a desire to be in control.

Bruce Grobbelaar
Goalkeeper (Liverpool FC)

This medium-sized handwriting tells us that the writer's imagination is never divorced from reality. He concentrates well and prefers to be practical and constructive. He lives very much for today and is quite a charmer, too. There is a lot of roundness in the writing, which indicates that he has his lazy days and also that he dislikes arguments or friction.

> *when MR Rea come out of his way to collect them. He was to take everything back to the Cayman Islands the next day to raise money for charity.*

However, because of the narrowness of some of the letters we see that he can become uptight and anxious under pressure. A Mr Nice-Guy who is proud of his achievements to date.

Gary Player
Golfer

> *Hope to have u one day.*
>
> *Sincerely,*
>
> *Gary Player.*

The right slant reveals this person's friendly and sociable nature. An emotionally healthy individual who is even-tempered, well-organised and clear-thinking. He has a keen mind and considerable executive ability. There is very good balance to the writing, showing he likes to give equal attention to all areas of his life. The additional starting strokes indicate caution and preliminary thinking before undertaking any task. The 'P' in 'Player' is whip-like and shows that he drives himself hard and always plays to win! He behaves exactly the same in private as in public.

Tessa Sanderson
Javelin thrower and heptathlete

The left slant here reveals a cautious lady who thinks before she acts. Her reversed 'd' in 'today' tells us that she is self-protective and dislikes being questioned about her moods or motives. The very angular lower loops show her high energy level, sporting interests and strong sex drive. The whole, however, suggests a lot of frustration in that she desires to be more progressive but is held back by negative past experiences which she cannot let go of. She is unsure of her self-image and finds criticism hard to take. She is both angry and confused but also very loyal and kind to her close friends.

Barry Sheen
Racing motorcyclist

This large handwriting speaks of a flamboyant person, who welcomes recognition. Part of the 'w' is eliminated,

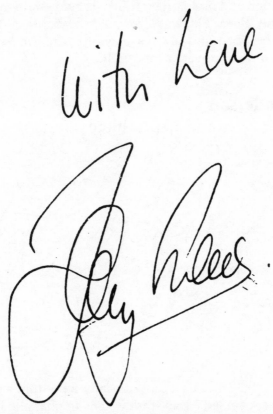

indicating that there is something in his day-to-day life that he finds unacceptable. The hook on the 'l' in 'love' hints at hoarding instincts. He is intelligent and has original ideas. The complicated and illegible signature reveals pride and also a lack of trust. He can be very suspicious of the moods and motives of others. The underline shows confidence and the full stop says 'Listen to me!'

Mark Spitz
Swimmer

There are some very unusual formations here, showing a great deal of originality in thought and action. Strong 't' crosses indicate the writer's will power and ability to get

things done. The pressure shows warmth and humour, but the endstroke on the 'z' reveals some disappointment in personal relationships. From the extension on the 'k' we can see his generosity, while the initial stroke instead of an 'M' is a sign of inquisitiveness and a thirst for knowledge.

STAGE AND SCREEN

Jane Asher
Actress and author (*Wish Me Luck*, etc.)

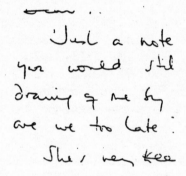

The handwriting of a reserved and spiritual individual. Great delicacy of feeling is revealed here. Her dislike of arguments or conflict is shown by the clean, light strokes. A refined person and a lover of all the arts. Very good word and line spacing showing planning and organising ability. This well-balanced script indicates good judgement and intuition. An articulate individual who speaks quietly, sincerely and positively, she sees essentials, acts upon them and makes little fuss or noise. Vulgarity has no appeal whatsoever. A culture vulture!

Warren Beatty
Film actor (*Bonnie and Clyde; Reds*)

A gentle, charming individual, as revealed by the roundness

[handwritten note:] We might have under-budget schedule! Love and thanks Warren

of the script. He is, however, quite persistent and progressive – note the right slant. The handwriting is mostly connected, showing his logical approach and his ability to work in a systematic manner, while the fullness indicates a colourful imagination and a flexibility in his attitude to others. Here is someone who is animated and vivacious. He has a relaxed nature and does not take life too seriously. Possessing a good visual memory, he is able to give a vivid description of an experience. On a more negative note, he may sometimes indulge in fantasies. A loving character with a great sense of humour. (*Shown slightly reduced.*)

Ingrid Bergman
Film actress (*For Whom the Bell Tolls*; *Casablanca*)

A person of high ideals, whose fellow humans seldom matched up to the high standards she set for them. The pressure is quite light, indicating a sensitive nature and a certain delicacy of feeling. She disliked rudeness or coarseness and was very much a lady. At times she allowed herself to be dominated by others with stronger personalities. She was tolerant, genial and spiritual. The narrowness of some of the letters speaks of a practical nature and a liking for order and tidiness. However, it also indicates her inhibitions

tone down the weaknesses
it wouldn't be honest.'
With all good wishes —

[signature]

in personal relationships. She was ambitious but procrastination, as shown by the 't' crosses that fail to cross the stems, did not permit her to achieve all her aims and desires.

Michael Caine
Film actor (*The Ipcress File; Educating Rita*)

Very connected writing, showing this person's logical, rational approach to everything. He has an enquiring mind but sometimes experiences difficulty in communicating just how intelligent he is. He has very good powers of concentration and a good memory for facts, although regarding day-to-day obligations he can be quite forgetful. This is the sharp handwriting of someone intense and rather rigid in his beliefs. The letters decrease in size at the ends of words, showing that he is manipulative and has a tendency to want things done his way. The 'i' dots pull very much to the right – a sign of impatience. A loyal man and protective of those close to him, he admires efficiency and does not suffer fools gladly. He is selective in his friendships.

Charlie (Sir Charles) Chaplin
Comedian, film actor and director
(*The Gold Rush; The Great Dictator*)

A surprisingly moody and oversensitive person who was very critical of both himself and others (seen by the sharpness of the strokes). The angles on the 't's indicate obstinacy and the desire to have his own way. His judgement of other people was good but he formed strong likes or dislikes based on first impressions. He kept his emotions very much under control and experienced difficulty in communicating intimately with anyone. Basically he was an austere, cleanliness-conscious individual who was never satisfied with his performance. However, he was very protective towards those he loved.

Joan Collins
Film and television actress (*The Bitch; Dynasty*)

A tremendously warm and sensual nature is shown here. The writer delights in all of her five senses, as seen by the pressure of the script. Her 'a's and 'o's are closed, showing discretion, and the full loops reveal her emotional nature. Her tying together of 'Joan' and 'Collins' tells us she likes to make the maximum use of her personality and will use her charm and wiliness to gain control. This is not a woman to argue with; she is very persistent, and she always plans for the future. She is frank, honest, direct and has a big ego. Her business acumen is considerable. She has a genuinely warm and friendly nature, welcomes a challenge and is very forward-thinking. Beauty delights her in all its shapes and forms.

Sean Connery
Film actor (James Bond in various films; *The Untouchables*)

This is the handwriting of a very charming individual, as shown by the roundness of the script. The pressure tells of a

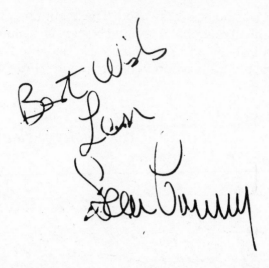

relaxed personality – someone who behaves the same in private as in public. He welcomes hard work, as indicated by the additional loops at the bases of 'Best' and 'Sean'. The slant wavers sometimes, so he can be moody but he quickly recovers. The uprightness tells us that his emotions are very much under control and that he is independent and self-reliant. One of his most attractive qualities is his dry wit. A delightful, loyal individual.

Sir Noël Coward
Dramatist, actor, composer and film director

This writer's strokes go in three directions, indicating a great sense of humour and a talent for mimicry. A very flamboyant signature, revealing his love of recognition and need to be noticed. Some pulls to the left show that he was nostalgic and liked to talk about the 'good old days'. He was a stubborn person and was not easily swayed. The beginning of the 'N' is a distinct phallic symbol. He could be very charming, but at other times irritable and standoffish. He delighted in gaiety and frivolity, but his reactions were frequently unpredictable.

Joan Crawford
Film actress (*Mildred Pierce; Whatever Happened to Baby Jane?*)

A lady with an alert, speedy mind, indicated by the slant to the right and the quick script. The very strong 't' crosses tell of her tenacity, persistence and desire to overcome all obstacles placed in her way. This was someone who never avoided a challenge; in fact it drove her to greater effort. She was restless, impatient and greedy, loved material possessions (note the very full lower zone) and constantly sought recognition. She was flamboyant, extroverted and attention-seeking. She could be uptight (some narrow letters) and moody, and often got her priorities wrong. The loops running into each other tell us she was accident prone but extremely energetic. An active and fulfilling sex life was important to her. The pointed underline speaks of a strong dislike of interference in her personal life. (*Shown slightly reduced.*)

Bette Davis

Film actress (*Jezebel; Whatever Happened to Baby Jane?*)

The rising lines show great enthusiasm for life. The rounded bases of the letters combined with the pointed tops (particularly on the 'm's) give a good clue that here was someone intellectually, but not emotionally, mature. Charm is in evidence, but behind an iron fist! The spiky 'p's suggest a very argumentative nature. She was a perfectionist who always liked to get her own way. Her 't' crosses fly to the right, showing intolerance of those less quick-thinking than herself. She had a love of the arts and of beauty, as seen by her Greek 'e's. Great impatience is shown; she wanted everything done yesterday.

Edward Fox

Film and television actor (*The Day of the Jackal; Edward and Mrs Simpson*)

Here we have a very clever combination of both angular and thread-like movements, showing that the writer is receptive to new ideas and thorough in everything he does. He is a perfectionist with a tendency to simplify issues. The starting stroke on the 'm' reveals scepticism, and the extremely small 'i' tells us he feels he has not achieved his full potential. He is

With my best wishes.

Yours sincerely. Edward Fox

articulate but cautious with words. An idealistic man who can appear very remote. The whole suggests he is dissatisfied with his success to date. Total accuracy is vital to him.

Liza Goddard
Stage and television actress (*Bergerac,* etc.)

Very light pressure and very large handwriting – this is in fact the perfect writing for the actor/actress who enjoys taking

Best wishes

Goddard x

on the role of another. It also indicates sensitivity and delicacy of feeling. These types are completely lacking in inhibition, but can sometimes allow others with a stronger personality to dominate them. They tend not to learn from past experiences but are invariably pleasant, charming and a joy to have around. This person welcomes and enjoys all the recognition she receives.

Nigel Hawthorne
Stage and television actor (*Yes, Minister; The Barchester Chronicles*)

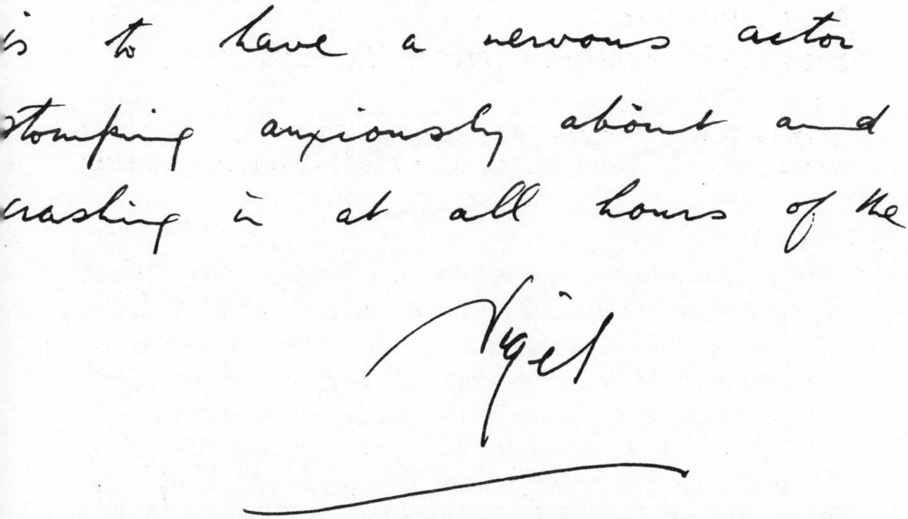

[handwritten text]

This is someone who works efficiently and with great precision, despite the fact that he is not naturally gifted with a lot of energy. It is a very right-slanting script which shows he enjoys giving vent to his feelings. Its connectedness tells of his good memory for factual detail. This is very intelligent, simplified handwriting, showing a direct and natural manner. His taste is quite austere and he likes to be surrounded by well-chosen objects. Vulgarity and loud colours are abhorrent to him. A lot of reserve is seen and the wide word spacing tells of the writer's need for privacy. He is very discriminating in his choice of friends.

Bernard Hepton
Television actor (*The Secret Army;
Tinker, Tailor, Soldier, Spy*)

*started well but
: appearing and there
in Eater. Let's hope*

Bernard Hepton

The pressure in this script tells of the writer's warmth and sense of humour. The slant varies slightly, which indicates that he can be moody: communicative one day, less so the next. The 'n's are broad, revealing his expansiveness in social situations. He enjoys travel and is kindly to the underdog. He does not like to be questioned about his movements and can be stubborn. The last letters of his words tend to be disconnected, suggesting that he often starts things he does not finish. Very little movement in the lower zone, showing a lack of interest in material things; not too much energy for sex but he may like a tipple!

Dustin Hoffman
Film actor (*The Graduate; Tootsie*)

A very determined individual who will leave no stone unturned in the pursuit of his own interests. A lot of mental energy and aggression is shown, as is an extremely positive attitude to life. His pen does not leave the paper, which indicates an angry obstinacy and persistence. His 't' cross shows imagination and the endstroke suggests he will keep at bay anyone who tries to hinder him. He is motivated by material gain and also has a strong sex drive. Both sceptical and critical, he will not hesitate to speak his mind. An achiever.

Princess Grace of Monaco
Film actress (as Grace Kelly)

Not a very inspiring signature for such a gracious lady. Its roundness shows her charm and the openings on the 'o's suggest oratory ability, but it is all rather copybook in style, indicating a preference for conventional and generally accepted standards of behaviour. Socially she was friendly but aloof. She was unadventurous but conscientious and co-operative, and had a very healthy respect for rules and regulations. Only in the 'G' of 'Grace' do we see any signs of self-assertion, but even these are quite mild. A lady who would have found difficulty in adapting to the changing face of modern society.

Sophia Loren
Film actress (*The Millionairess;*
The Cassandra Crossing)

Mental agility is revealed here by the directness of the

strokes. The loops are full, showing the writer can be very emotional, and the majority of the 'o's are knotted, suggesting a secretive nature. However, this is a lady who comes straight to the point and says exactly what she has to say. She does not suffer fools gladly and because of the size of her handwriting we know she enjoys acclaim and recognition. The signature is somewhat illegible, confirming her desire to keep her innermost thoughts to herself. An individual who is difficult to get to know but always charming on a superficial level.

Joanna Lumley
Actress and television personality (*The New Avengers*, etc.)

The very strong, thick pressure here shows a lady of warmth and humour. The connectedness of her signature indicates that she is logical, while the knot on the 'e' tells us she can be guarded and secretive. From the size of the writing we can see that she needs recognition, is very ambitious and dislikes spending long periods of time alone. The pointed tops on the 'm' show an enquiring mentality; this is someone who likes to have answers even to the inexplicable. The large, swinging loop on the 'y' shows a high energy level and sexual adventurousness.

Virginia McKenna
Film actress and animal-rights campaigner
(*Carve Her Name with Pride; Born Free*)

[handwritten text]

A charming, delightful lady with great delicacy of feeling. This is a sensitive person who has no time in her life for anger, friction or aggressiveness. She has definite ideas and will work hard to achieve her aims, but in a direct, honest and matter-of-fact way. She is never two-faced and behaves the same with everyone. The simplicity of her strokes shows efficiency and a love of culture. The little crossing on the 'y' tells us she is very romantic and is in love with the idea of being in love.

Marilyn Monroe
Film actress (*Lets Make Love; Some Like It Hot*)

This right-slanting script shows someone who loved communicating with others and was quite modern in her thinking. She was enthusiastic, restless and filled with nervous energy. She loved activity and was driven by strong sexual urges which could at times dominate her life. These are shown by the long lower loops running into the words below. When these urges overtook her, she was like a child and wanted instant gratification. The long endstroke on 'seeing' suggests that she felt threatened. She was a very

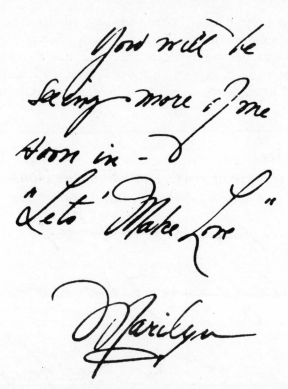

warm, affectionate lady but all the ink-filled ovals tell of explosive outbursts and a tendency to excess, not just in matters of sex, but in food and drink too. The very involved 'M' in 'Marilyn' indicates absorption with self and great vanity. The lack of pressure on the right-hand side of the 'l' reveals her great insecurity about the future.

Pat Phoenix
Television actress (Elsie Tanner in *Coronation Street*)

A rhythmic type of signature, showing someone who tried to find smooth solutions to difficult problems. Some angular movements in the small letters indicate that underneath a soft front was quite a tough lady. The rounded tops to the capitals show a protectiveness towards those close to her and the ability to project her own personality and use it to the maximum effect. Some compulsiveness is seen, as is determination and intelligence. A mixture here of strength and vulnerability.

Vincent Price
Film actor (*House of Wax; The Fall of the House of Usher*)

A very interesting script; the narrow letters and the wide spacing between them clearly indicate that although this writer is outwardly an extrovert character, underneath he is uptight, somewhat introverted and very cautious when expressing his feelings. The tick stroke at the beginning of 'suddenly' shows him clinging to old ideas, finding difficulty in looking to the future. Humour of a dry nature is shown, and he likes to take the lead and to stand out in a crowd, but he is not too comfortable with himself. The whip-like movements indicate a slightly cruel and controlling nature, but also an artistic one.

Dave Prowse
Film and television actor (Darth Vader in *Star Wars*)

The very large writing of someone who is a great attention seeker, loves working in the public eye and is at his best when being observed. It is quite an angular script, revealing a lot of determination and mental aggression. The long starting strokes leading in to 'Darth' and 'Dave' show someone who thrives on a platform and needs an audience to come alive. The large capitals also indicate a lot of self-confidence and feelings of pride in his achievements. The reverse underline is a sign that he likes to keep his family and children away from the public eye. A capable man, who will give his all in order to succeed in whatever career he takes on. Many leadership qualities are shown. (*Shown slightly reduced.*)

Oliver Reed
Film actor (*Women in Love; Castaway*)

The rightward slant shows this writer's love of communication, but as the majority of his 'a's and 'o's are closed we can see that he will communicate with others only when he wants to. The 'd's always swing to the left, indicating that he is very self-protective and will always have a quick, ready reply and a good excuse for his misdemeanours. There is a lot of humour and bravado to the script, but because of the very high and firm 't' crossings we find a man who is protective towards family and friends alike. He produces a strong, unusually shaped 'p' in 'pleased', showing he can be sexually athletic. His letters vary in size, giving a good clue to mood changes and variations in his own feelings of self-worth. An attractive, larger-than-life character who would be difficult to pin down.

Burt Reynolds
Film actor (*Deliverance; Smokey and the Bandit*)

The large capital letters here show pride, ambition and the desire for recognition. The full loops tell us he is an emotional man who becomes deeply involved in any part he plays. He is very logical, as shown by the connectedness of the script, and will become irritated if interrupted during the course of his work. It is also an aesthetic script, indicating his love of beauty and beautiful surroundings. This is a romantic man with a great sense of humour. The long, extended endstrokes show his discrimination when forming close relationships. He values greatly those whom he trusts.

Frank Sinatra
Singer and film actor (*From Here to Eternity; High Society*)

A flowing signature which reveals the writer's easy co-ordination. An intelligent man who can be both manipulative and diplomatic. He faces problems head-on and is a good, speedy decision maker. He dislikes procrastination and can be very impatient. The 'S', rather like an egg timer, tells us that he has a strong dislike of the ageing process! The reversed loop on the 'k' in 'Frank' speaks of his rebellious-ness and occasional desire to shock.

Terence Stamp
Film actor (*Billy Budd; Far from the Madding Crowd*)

The very thread-like writing gives a great clue to this man's

restless and curious nature. He has a hunger for new experiences but finds difficulty in communicating his thoughts and feelings to others. He is a gentle and wandering spirit and, like his signature, is either riding on the crest of a wave or quietly pondering. He will seek the companionship of original and imaginative people and will not allow himself to give way to anger or aggression. He views the world from a wide perspective.

Elizabeth Taylor
Film actress (*Cat on a Hot Tin Roof; Who's Afraid of Virginia Woolf?*)

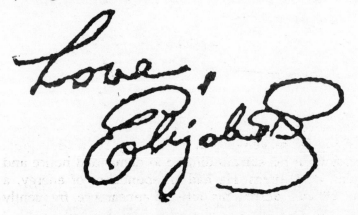

This rising signature clearly shows the writer's professional ambition. The swinging 'L' in 'Love' reveals her charisma, charm and sense of humour, while the inflated 'E' in 'Elizabeth' indicates a need to attract attention and a love of public adoration. The 'z' shows a strong sex drive and the extension on the 'e' in 'Love' says that she is generous and likes to give to those she loves. She can be quite vulgar and enjoys storytelling, often embroidered for good effect. The pressure of the writing tells of her warmth, but it is also erratic, showing varying energy levels. A lot of emotion is seen here, but she is also a great flirt.

John Wayne
Film actor (*Stagecoach; True Grit*)

*this note
enduring*

*Warm regards
John Wayne*

This was a very domineering and aggressive man, as shown by the angular movements in the writing. He made a great impression on his surroundings and demanded notice and attention at all times. He had an abundance of energy, a strong will and, despite his outward appearance, frequently felt uptight, cautious and ill-at-ease. Sarcasm and a cynical attitude are in evidence, as is the ability to subdue others with a few well-chosen words. His sex drive was strong but so was his sense of dissatisfaction and frustration.

Barbara Windsor
Film actress (*Carry on Cabby*, etc.)

There are very small spaces between the words in this script,

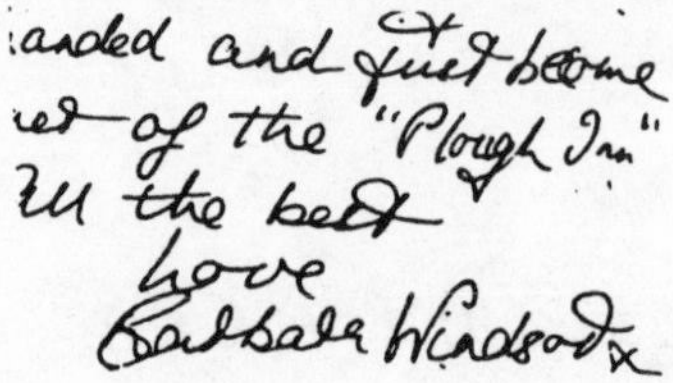

[handwritten note]
...anded and just become
...et of the "Plough Inn"
in the best
love
Barbara Windsor x

indicating that here is someone who will crowd others for attention. She needs closeness and affection but can experience some difficulty in returning such warmth. She knots a lot of her letters, telling of her inflexibility, while the 'g' in 'Plough' suggests a great deal of sexual vanity. She actually enjoys displaying her physical attributes and her motto is, 'If you've got it, flaunt it!' A Peter-Pan lady with a great sense of humour. She is a good mimic too.

THE ROYAL FAMILY

Her Majesty Queen Elizabeth II

The Queen's regal signature shows us that she is comfortable with her position. She is very clear-thinking – note the simplification of the letter formations – and her firm 't' cross shows a strong will. The unadorned capital 'E' indicates her refinement, gentleness and love of cultural pursuits. It is slightly narrow handwriting, suggesting that she experiences some difficulty in relaxing. The loops show thoroughness and controlled emotion. She is idealistic and demands a lot of herself.

Her Majesty Queen Elizabeth the Queen Mother

This large, imposing signature is much as one would expect from royalty, and shows the Queen Mother's regal and leadership qualities. Its clarity speaks of directness and the steady baseline reveals her reliability and emotional stability. The leftward pull on the capital 'E' indicates self-confidence, self-reliance and independence, and also shows her motherly instincts. The whole indicates her love of, and comfort with, pomp and ceremony. This signature is very similar to that of the Queen, and we can see that both writers are happy in their roles.

HRH The Duke of Edinburgh

Prince Philip's signature is written with very firm, straight strokes, showing his direct, no-nonsense attitude. 'If you have something to say, say it,' is his motto. He has a strong dislike of waffle and time wasting and does not suffer fools gladly. He can be both impatient and critical, and is very logical, so appeals to him must be based on facts not emotion. He has high ideals and sets high standards for himself and others, as shown by the tall upper-zone letters. He is very curious – note the high 'i' dots – and has good powers of observation. Great loyalty is shown and also a high energy level. The leanness of the writing tells us that he is seldom interested in anything that does not serve a useful purpose.

HRH The Prince of Wales

This writing, which slants to the left, shows caution and extreme sensitivity. Prince Charles takes offence easily and his emotions are not to be tampered with. There is a strong mother influence and we can see that he experiences great difficulty in accepting change or progress. He can be charming in social situations but finds it hard to express emotion. His tightly knotted 'o's reveal that he is sometimes secretive and crafty. He likes his own way, shows a lot of independence and invariably keeps those close to him at arm's length. He has a fair degree of energy and always pushes himself to the limit. As a lover he can be self-centred and somewhat unadventurous.

HRH The Princess of Wales

This is the handwriting of one who lives very much for today; whatever activity she is involved in at a given moment is undertaken gracefully and with interest. She is very charming, as illustrated by the roundness of the script. The rather large 'a's say that she can be quite possessive in her relationships with friends and partner alike. It is important to her to be needed and she cares what others think of her. She is quick-thinking but not particularly original. The broadness of the writing shows a need for freedom in thought and action. It is very important to her to communicate openly with others. Undoubtedly the greatest difficulty she will experience in her marriage to Prince Charles is his lack of readiness to relate closely and intimately with her. Outward displays of affection are also necessary to her.

HRH The Princess Royal

Dear Ann,

Thank you so much for your invitation — I'd love to come on Dec. 18th, perhaps nearer the date

Yours sincerely,

Anne

The handwriting of a no-nonsense lady. She speaks her mind but surprisingly is more sensitive to criticism than she would ever let the world know (shown by the looped 'd's). She will actually stew about slights or insults but will never admit this to anyone. She has a tough exterior but a soft core! Very firm strokes tell us she is a dedicated, thorough achiever who gives her all to anything she undertakes. The very tall capitals show how she sets out with a high degree of confidence but invariably feels dissatisfied with the end result. The uprightness of the script shows a loyal individual who values family and close friends greatly. A good, strong sex drive is indicated by the deep, long strokes in the lower zone.

Captain Mark Phillips

This fairly small signature with compensating large capitals reveals a reasonably outgoing person who is outwardly confident but basically rather reserved and happiest when working by himself. His tall letters are a sign of idealism, and the gaps between the letters show a great deal of intuition and perception. His ideas are very personal. He can be critical of others but has little insight into his own feelings. He may at times be rather anti-social. The narrow 'p' in 'Phillips' shows repressed sexuality, but the rising signature and small underline reveal cautious optimism.

HRH The Duke of York

The rather old-fashioned capital 'A' shows Prince Andrew's respect for tradition, and the rounded baseline his ability to remain charming in social situations. Three-way movements indicate a sense of humour, but the reversed small 'r' tells us that he can sometimes be touchy or oversensitive. He is independent by nature and will make his own decisions. A very loyal and steadfast individual who is protective towards his family and friends. The broadness of the 'w' indicates ambition and courage, while the pressure shows a warm and loving person who likes surprising his partner.

HRH The Duchess of York

Like her signature, the Duchess is bouncy and plunges enthusiastically into anything she undertakes. She is

Sarah Ferguson.

observant, as shown by the gap after the capital 'S'. More intuitive than other members of the royal family, she follows her instincts and can size up people and situations very quickly. Her basic desire is to offer the hand of friendship to those who wish to take it. A very pleasant individual, not always the most tactful but sincere and honest. She is warm and loving, has a great sense of humour and does not take life too seriously. A good partner and ideally suited to her husband.

HRH The Prince Edward

Edward

Quite a broad signature, indicating someone who needs space in which to spread himself and feels confined in small areas. Prince Edward can be a little shy but is nonetheless drawn towards people. The variable pressure suggests mood swings, and the small 'x' in the capital 'E' gives us a clue to his critical nature. He is quite charming but has a tendency to depression. He does not seek the limelight and is more comfortable with people he knows well. He communicates fluently but in a quiet manner.

HRH The Princess Margaret

The second descending stroke on the 'M' tells us of Princess Margaret's stubborn nature and her desire to get her own way. The middle-zone letters show how charming she can be, but they also indicate secretiveness. She dislikes being questioned closely and the looped 't' suggests that she can be sensitive and take offence easily. The removed 't' cross reveals impatience and, at times, a very condescending attitude. The firm, strong underline says, 'I am a princess, do not forget it.'

HRH Princess Alexandra

A very direct, straightforward attitude is shown in this signature. The large letters tell us that Princess Alexandra enjoys her prominent position in public life, but the 'x' suggests she can, at times, feel weighed down by responsibility. There is humour in the 'd' movement and also a love of music. The simplicity of the 'A' shows efficiency and cultural awareness, while the combination of connected and disconnected letters reveals a good balance between logical and intuitive thinking, which enables her to fulfil many of her desires and ambitions.

TELEVISION PERSONALITIES

Sir Alastair Burnet
Newscaster

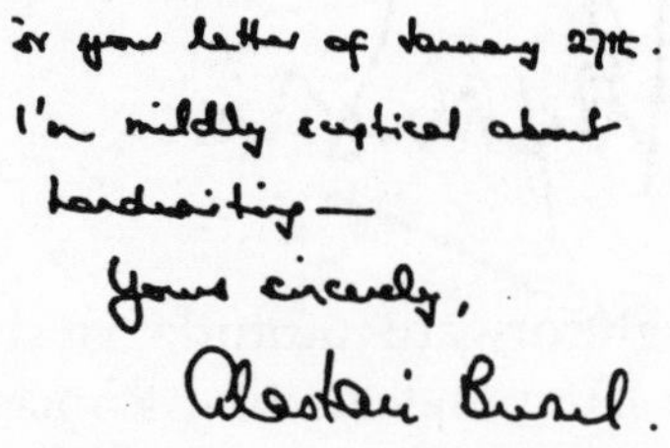

[handwritten note:]

> in your letter of January 27th.
> I'm mildly sceptical about
> handwriting —
>   Yours sincerely,
>   Alastair Burnet.

A simple, straightforward, balanced script indicating honesty, integrity and directness. The writer likes to give equal attention to all areas of his life and is a very good judge of character. The rather small personal pronoun 'I' tells us he is a modest individual who needs, on occasions, to spend time quietly alone. The baseline is extremely regular, showing utter reliability and emotional stability. The clear word and line spacing indicate planning and organising ability. Negatively, he can be inflexible, a little too rigid in his views and somewhat condescending.

Judith Chalmers
Presenter, *Wish You Were Here*

The large size of this script, with its rounded baseline, tells of a charming, pleasant and natural individual who delights in whatever task she is involved in. This is full handwriting (taking up a lot of space), showing someone who is flexible,

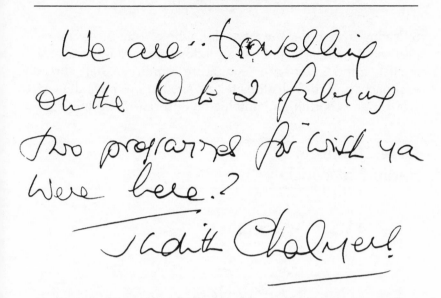

easily animated and full of life. She is a good communicator, as indicated by the right slant, and she puts herself out to be pleasant to other people. She has a love of the spectacular and is greedy for new experiences. She is inclined to be extravagant, but is a very hard worker. At times she can be overemotional and a little impatient, but the writing in general shows a delightful personality and one who is protective towards her friends and family. (*Shown slightly reduced.*)

Anna Ford
Journalist and broadcaster

An angular script, showing mental energy and directness. This lady is firm, determined and knows what she wants from life. She can become very impatient with time wasters or anyone less than efficient. A stubborn streak is shown by the 'p' in 'pockets'. There are some breaks here between letters, revealing intuition, but, on the whole, she likes to be presented with facts and has a predominantly analytical and logical mind. Her firm signature confirms her direct approach, and the full stops tell us she likes to have the last word. She is both highly intelligent and self-disciplined.

Derek Jameson
Radio 2 disc jockey

The slight left slant to this writing tells of the writer's cautious and sensitive nature. Left slanters are capable of maintaining a very polished front and can be charming in social situations whilst remaining emotionally aloof. There are many angular movements in the script, showing high intelligence and versatility. The sharpness tells us he is articulate and also quite intense, while the small size indicates an academic mentality. The writing as a whole suggests a disciplined personality and the underline again confirms his quiet confidence. The full stop says, 'I like the last word!'

Dr Hilary Jones
Television doctor, TV-am

The small handwriting of the scientist – note the accurately placed 'i' dots. The left slant shows he is cautious and considered in his opinions and speech. The smallness of the script tells us he is quite a shy and reserved individual, and from the large 'O' in 'Once' we can see that while he likes to

Once upon a time a family practitioner wrote said 'Giz a job'. programmes waved his a Hey presto!

emerge in the public eye, he is equally happy to retire to his clinic afterwards. The 'm's and 'n's reveal an enquiring mentality. One would not be surprised to find him involved in research at some stage of his life.

Lorraine Kelly
Presenter, TV-am

This lady's very large writing tells us she loves working in the public eye, welcomes recognition and is happiest when engaged in large-scale projects. As there are only a few words to each line we know she is an extravagant gift buyer, both for

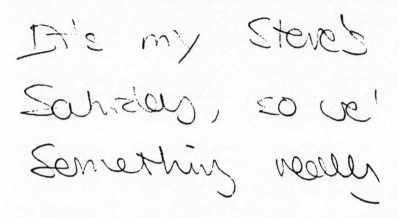

herself and others. The lines rise slightly, showing her optimism and enthusiasm for everything she does, but from the occasional variations in the slant we can detect odd bouts of moodiness. The capital 'I' in 'It's' shows confidence and, at the time of writing, her lower loops reveal her as an adventurous but spasmodic lover.

Robert Kilroy-Silk
Presenter, *Kilroy*

These small letters of regular and even size indicate conscientiousness and consistency. The 'w' written like an 'm' shows an enquiring mind, and the whole speaks of charm, kindness and friendliness. It is important to this writer to be liked and he does his utmost to achieve that end. The printed 's' shows his love of reading and his large capitals his desire for public acclaim. The very small 't' crossings indicate that he can experience difficulty in overcoming day-to-day obstacles.

Sue Lawley
Television and radio interviewer

Many apologies for not replying to you sooner! Here are my few lines of hand-writing as you request.

Best wishes —

Sue Lawley.

The very clearly written signature shows us that there is no pretentiousness to this lady. Her intuitive qualities are seen in the disconnectedness of the script, which, combined with very balanced zones, indicates directness and good judgement. This is the writing of an emotionally stable individual who likes plain talking. Some of her 'i' dots pull to the right, showing signs of impatience, but the whole suggests she welcomes a challenge, does not seek the approval of others and is a good, speedy decision maker. Her personal relationships could be a little difficult as she is extremely independent, seen by the uprightness of the script, and may expect those close to her to understand her feelings without giving them a clue as to what is going on in her head.

Little and Large
Comedians

Syd Little
A large but narrow script with a leftward slant reveals a cautious, nervous and exacting personality – one that is

rarely satisfied with his own efforts. He is frequently on the defensive and his unusual split 'd' tells of a rebellious streak. He is an ambitious, proud man who gives his all to anything he undertakes.

Eddie Large

Eddie Large (signature)

The decreasing letter sizes at the ends of the names give an indication as to this writer's tact and diplomacy, while the pressure, slightly heavier than that of his partner, suggests that it is he who can best inject humour and warmth into situations. The 'd's in 'Eddie' show humour and thoroughness, but the low cross on the 'g' tells of sexual disappointment.

Bob Monkhouse
Comedian and game-show host

treat (I added a couple of old shows). Will be in touch again soon. Have a great trip or, if you've already been & come back. Welcome home! All the best ... (signature)

This writer shows genuine warmth and is very good company, but he is also a man who knows what he wants and how to get it. A great deal of personal magnetism is seen by the uprightness of the script, together with independence, inner strength and the ability to control his emotions. The ornate capitals are the sign of the bluffer and showman, one who thrives on recognition. A challenge appeals to him and drives him to greater effort, and he is also big-hearted and enjoys new experiences. Some lovely, large 'g' loops indicate his interest in material things and his prowess as a lover – he's very adventurous!

Claire Rayner
Agony aunt and author

This speedy script tells us that the writer is always in a hurry, wants everything yesterday and tries to achieve too much. It shows a very quick mind and one that is stimulated by a challenge. However, the trailing at the ends of her words suggests she can be a bit of a slave driver with a low tolerance level, and her 't' crosses tell us she is sometimes arrogant and condescending. Gaps between letters show both her critical and literary ability, and one would not be surprised if she occasionally came up with a brilliant idea. Her personal pronoun 'I' reveals that no matter what she achieves, she always wants to do better and is never completely satisfied with her own efforts. Many of the straight strokes to the 'y's state, sexually, 'I eat when I am hungry!'

Anneka Rice
Presenter, *Challenge Anneka*

This is speedy handwriting indicating a quick mind. From the tall upper-zone movements, we can see that the writer is idealistic, ambitious and self-motivated. The words are too close together, though, showing a tendency to crowd others for attention; she is demanding of their time whilst not always prepared to give of her own. Impatience, observance and a critical nature are in evidence. However, she finds it difficult to take criticism herself. She is a poor delegator and feels that if you want something done properly, you must do it yourself. She is very intelligent with a good sense of timing, as shown by the firm, straight downstrokes. The concave 't' crosses hint at self-indulgence and some fickleness, but the whole suggests someone who is determined to succeed.

Jimmy (Sir James) Savile
Philanthropist; presenter, *Jim'll Fix It*

This signature almost speaks for itself – a great sense of humour and fun and a love of dollars and pounds. The rounded 'i' dot shows he is also in love with himself and the large size states he really enjoys big projects and is very ambitious. He connects almost all his letters, so he is logical enough to turn his dreams into actions. A larger-than-life character – quite sensual too. He does not care what anyone thinks of him and invariably goes his own sweet way.

Jimmy Tarbuck
Comedian

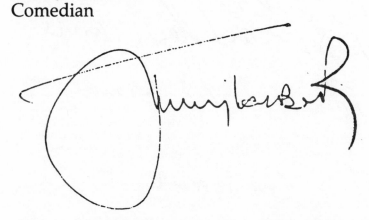

A great deal of ambition is seen in the exaggerated capitals of this signature. This is the writing of a natural showman who welcomes all the attention he receives. Humour runs throughout (three-way strokes) and the overlarge 'k' in 'Tarbuck' shows a rebellious and sometimes tactless streak. 'Watch me, I'm great!' is the statement he's making here. The straight stroke on the 'y' reveals he can be a selfish lover, but the huge 'T' cross shows his protectiveness towards his family. He is a show-off but happy that way. He feels very uncomfortable when faced with arguments or conflict of any type.

Chris Tarrant
Capital Radio disc jockey

Silly exercises.

pen off the desk

paper and then write

it... I mean,

Chris Tarrant

A right-slanting, lively script, indicating a very bouncy, jovial character who thoroughly enjoys being in the public eye. He thrives on attention. Very firm 't' crosses show his ability to overcome day-to-day obstacles, and considerable business acumen is also found. His firm, straight strokes show his good sense of timing and his three-way movements confirm that he possesses a delightful sense of humour. The personal pronoun 'I' is the sign of an independent decision maker, and the whole shows innovative thinking and the capacity to succeed in whatever area he wishes to follow. He just doesn't let go! His left leg gives him some trouble.

Terry Wogan
Television interviewer

Here's hoping that you won't draw a blank on me!

[signature: Terry Wogan]

Charm oozes from this writing but it is not always genuine; this is a man who can be charming to his worst enemy. Starting strokes before the letters suggest that he likes to think things through before making a decision, and the hook at the beginning of 'that' reveals that once he gets an idea into his head it can be very difficult to make him change his mind. The balanced nature of the script shows he is a good judge of character and can size up situations very quickly, but the capital 'R's in the middle of words suggest he can get his priorities wrong and can behave quite rebelliously under pressure. Humour appears everywhere, as indicated by the three-way strokes, but the pointed underline to his signature shows he can become angry with those who invade his privacy. He tends to resist change and feels more secure with what is tried and trusted. (*Shown slightly reduced.*)

Mike Yarwood
Impersonator

The pointed tops to the 'm's in this script show an enquiring and critical mind. The writer is very demanding of himself and will settle for nothing less than perfection. The heavy, accurately placed 'i' dots confirm just how attentive to detail he is, and the loop at the base of the 'b' is another sign of his dedication to his work. Because of the intertwining of the letters, we see that he can get his priorities wrong and is somewhat accident prone. The signature suggests he displays more confidence outwardly than is indeed the fact, and the pull of the loops to the left tells us that he relies on a partner for emotional strength. A very talented man who does not really believe it! The little ticks on the capital 'T' and 'Y' reveal that he has difficulty in letting go of ideas from the past.

INDEX